My Walls Crumbled Down

ISBN 978-0-9858029-2-9

I

My Walls Crumbled Down

By Ralph L. Watts

I have always appreciated great Christian Speakers.

They somehow inspired a belief in me that made me believe they were in control.

It had got to the point where whenever I see them I see God.

This book is written explaining how I let my feelings for Christian Preachers crumbled my wall.

Contents

Chapter 1

The Seeing Eye

In the beginning my seeing eyes were always there to see and give me confidence that what we see is true. Too many times we see things and automatically put reference to what we see.

These references what cause mistakes in our daily life. We do not want to designate the time to try to understand reasons why we see what we see.

Whenever I turn on the television set I look for special people who in my mind were the living words. Whatever they would say I did not question it. I felt like they had the authority to do almost everything.

I had a wall built around these people. To me they were more than an inspiration source. What I seen in them is what I believed. Well, that is not so true.

These people I am speaking of are national known. I had this wall of belief that a shadow of dough was missing. No one could tell me this was not the wall for me.

I sung and prayed along with them advocating the Word was with us and not anything could separate us.

One day the Devil caused trouble in my life. The trouble came without warning which caught me at the most bondable time of my life.

I was in the process of writing the book "The Assassination of a Mind". Many publishers wanted me to publish with them.

There were also these subsidy publishers

who wanted my manuscript. Then the book printers got involved. The information I was receiving were very confusing.

Not having the experience I began to make mistakes. These mistakes were costing me plenty. A good friend Chellie McTeer came to my rescue and loan me some money to help.

A few days later my car broke down on the interstate. Once again Chellie McTeer came to my rescue. She hope me get my car to a repair shop had my car repaired.

Two days later I went to my daughter birthday party. After the birthday party my family went to a ball game. I started to go home.

On the way home I stop for a soda. I got the soda and returned to my car. Again the car would not start. I was in the wrong neighborhood and I just knew things were not good for me.

A few guys gave me a boost trying to get it going but were unsuccessful. It began to darken and the neighborhood hoodlums began to gather. I could see in their eyes I was going to be their prey.

I tried to call my children and grandchildren. They would not answer their phones. I felt a sense of helplessness.

I realized at one point this is a test and what shall I do? I sit quietly and prayed.

I prayed and prayed. These were some real and honest prayers. I could not rely on my television set for help. It was not there but I continued to pray.

After an hour of praying my phone ranged. It was Chellie McTeer on the other end. Man was I glad to hear her voice. I told her where I was and she came. I said to myself God answered my prayers.

Immediately she told me I had to get out this neighborhood. She called a wrecker and had my car tolled to a shop. I was so grateful for her help.

I asked to take me to my daughter's house to spend the night. She took me there twice until we realized she was not coming home.

Chellie offered to take me to her sister house to spend the night. I did not want to go but I had no other choice. I spent the night at her sister's house.

Early the next morning Chellie came over to assist and help me get my car repaired. Once again Chellie loan me more money for my car.

I then and only then realized God answered if you ask him. You have to pray your prayer because your life and problems are different from everyone else.

God is blessing Chellie and I am really going to make sure she gets all her money back.

As I write this book my food supply is about zero. I have only three Ramon noodles left. Even though I have not received any other help I am trusting God will deliver me.

The Wall I had was shaky because I could not contact the people who I worshipped with. I had to rely on my own faith that God will deliver me.

Chapter 2

Getting Help

My next step is trying to get help. First I will contact the television ministries. I know they are able to help me:

I had a lot of confidence in Joel Osteen. I listen to most of his broadcasts and praised God along with him. I am sure he will help me.

I wrote to him asking for help. I sent all the proving evident to substantiate my story. I just knew I could get help from him which I believe is a man of God.

I waited a long time for his answer. The answer never came but, he did send my materials back and included one of his booklets. (Thirty (30) thoughts for Victorious Living)

I grab this booklet looking thru for a dollar. Just a dollar so I could go to the Dollar store and buy some Ramon noodles. This dollar would provide five (5) meals. The dollar was not there.

I explained to him in my letter that I was deeply in need. I guess he did not understand my condition. I would have been grateful if he would have placed just a dollar in his booklet.

My wall crumbled from around him. I do not understand how someone could not help another in need. I am a poor man but I always tried to help someone in need.

I wrote to T. D. Jakes asking for help. I did get an answer from his office. They asked if I had a testimony. I told them I needed help and my condition was critical. I did not hear from them again. Again my wall crumbled from around him.

Here are others that I tried to get help and without any answers.

Keith Jenkins at T. D. Jakes, Rev. Al Sharpie, Governor Deal, Jessie Jackson, Ken Amira, NAN National Headquarters, Black Press,

Haki Madhubuti and Tom Joiner mail sent to Rev. Al Sharpie.

Out of all the people above you would say that someone, just one would give some help.

When I contacted Georgia State for help I just knew my problems were over. I did not receive any help from them. Therefore

I wrote the book "The Assassination of a Mind" It explains all the problems I had trying to get help from Georgia. Help never came.

What do you do when you ask your State for help? There is no help for you. If you ask all the people you know are able to help and will not? This is a feeling that no one want to experience.

I felt terribly bad about myself and everyone around me. I felt useless, helpless and scared to death.

Some people will set back and say "He should have done this or that". That is not a good answer; you are in a condition that anyone can fall in that need help.

I went to ones I knew were able to help. I also recognize that God help come through others. I know they should give as generously as God does.

Now my mind began to wonder about other things in my life and this world.

I was very depressed thinking about my conditions. Why am I having so many Problems?

The answer immediately came to me. The Devil is taking over this country. He is causing problems in everyone's life.

I understand how the Devils took over America. He placed ungodly leaders in specific places to serve him. They are the ones that lust for money.

Under our ungodly leadership this nation no longer lived under the blanket of God's word. They have destroyed most of our religious way of living.

The rich people who steal millions and most get away. The ones that get caught get a slap on the wrist. The poor get sent to prison for a few hundred dollars.

We have lost two generation of children. The Devil gets them young. Since there are no prayers in school he gives them guns to shoot their teachers.

What I had to understand under God's blanket we all have a purpose, a chosen destiny and fellowship in the name of God.

This world today is sinful and insecure. We must turn to Jesus for hope, understanding and peace.

What God sees when he looks down on America? He sees a corrupt, full of hate and an unjust nation. A nation that is sinful and unwilling to serve and be faithful to our Heavenly Father.

Look around you or the news on your television set. God does not like all this ugliness that the American people do.

You might say I do not do those things. You are wrong, very wrong. You voted for these leaders to make laws for us to abide by. Yes you are a part of what is happening in this country.

What these leaders want is to get on the news to make you believe them. All these leaders want is to make their pockets fat.

They are not there to help you. If you don't believe me just ask for help. They will tell how to get help but to help you themselves is out.

If I approach a leader with lots of money I would not have any trouble bringing forth my idea whether it good or bad. Money is proven to be a driving factor in providing any ungodly faction. We must understand the above and not put our trust in man.

As my walls crumble I could see all the ugliness behind their doors. A small group gets together with their ideas to make millions. These millions are made from the poor for their livelihood.

Here you have a situation where the poor get poorer and the rich get richer. To get help from them will be somewhere they want to show in the news they are very helpful. What a price for us to pay for our vote.

Our vote got most of us in situation where Satan can rule over you. Let me give you an idea what I am speaking of. Satan places certain people in place to make rules Satan can control. One day their walls will crumble.

As the years passed I saw something in our laws that were causing our crime rate to rise. It is the Felon law. All our felons are treated the same. They cannot get a good job hold a political office or even vote. They are excluded from the mainstream of our society.

A few years ago in the news was a candidate running for Governor from his prison cell? I said to myself, "Wait a minute! How a person run for Governor in prison and a non-violent felon cannot vote". There is something wrong with this picture. Then I realize the Lawmakers made a law that would cancel a person from returning to a normal lifestyle.

A young man commit a non-violent felon should be able to return to a normal lifestyle within five, no more than ten years. This gives him a second chance to make a good life for himself. At least there is a chance of hope is available if he takes this choice.

There is a man I know in his seventies. He had a non-violent felon in his young years.

He told me of the struggles, hardships and embarrassments he carried his whole life.

Every good job he applied for and told of his felon he could not qualify. Most times he had to work two jobs to make up for one.

Most men return to crimes because there is no hope. What they need is hope to stay out of trouble and a normal lifestyle is guaranteed. The Law needs to be changed to give our young people hope in case they do make a mistake. This law should only apply to non-violent crimes.

Why this law is this way? We voted ungodly people in office and they cannot think. To make things righteous we need the knowledge from God.

If we get the Devils out God would bless this country. He would cool the summers, warm the winters and hold the tornados.

He would bless our children and give them respect. The children today I see wearing ugly clothes with their underwear showing. There is never a "No Sir or Yes Sir" no respect in sight. Never-the-less we are responsible for this happening.

We sit back and accept all the ugliness the Americans do. Are we guilty? Yes you are: If you are an American voter you are guilty and responsible.

The fight between Republicans and Democrats are very frightening. Just in the last election; a new elected person stated "His voyage is getting rid of the President". I could not believe I heard that. If anyone felt that way he should be ashamed to say it. The people voted him in and no one question his statement. I watch television and I hear Ministers giving ugly statements about our President. Yes, I believe Satan have taken over.

How in the world do you expect a country to b successful with these types of attitudes?

The prayers left our schools set a stage for the Devils to reign. Listen to the news; every stati mention disasters. The Judges are giving uneq sentences to certain people.

God have been good to this Country. The goodness of forgiveness and holiness is gone. There is nothing left but a very few that understand what to expect from this type of governing body. They are not surprise because they are saved and know what happens to governments when the people elect devils to guide them. READ YOUR BIBLE!!!

I truly wish that this country could regain her strength again. It would almost impossible to get rid of the Devils the people have elected. They think they are our boss and we let them.

Chapter 3

Keeping your walls from Crumbling.

One way to get started is raising our children.

Raising children today is like breeding criminals. Parents are not supposed to whip their children. They are supposed to beg their children to do what is asked of them.

I am so proud and grateful my parents whipped, spanked and scared the hell out of me if I did anything wrong. It made a good person out of me. All the older people I spoke with agreed. Kids these days find out they can do anything and get away with it. If the parents disagree, too bad kids will call the law.

As I look down the streets; what do you see? You see young boys walking with their pants hanging showing their nasty dirty underwear. They have artificial hair all over their head like a moose. Why don't the parents tell them that these things are ugly, nasty and not becoming to decent men?

Why don't the parents teach them to dress

neat? Why doesn't the city make laws to make this dress against the law? Is it because our Lawmakers have kids or grandchildren dressing this way?

If our lawmakers were godly people they would not allow this to happen. We are supposed to judge ourselves and children by God's law and not man.

If America does not get on board with the word of God her world is going to crumble.

This is something I am not guessing; all you

have to do is read your bible. Do not blame anything on anyone but yourself. You are the voter and you wanted the Devil to run your country.

How and why I say things like this?

Look around you; do you see any of God laws being broken? Do you see men, women and what else doing what thus said the Lord? Open your mind and think; God is not going to continue letting us go this way much longer.

My world crumbled again because one

Judge made a terrible mistake. He judge for man and not God. This mistake caused me to lose all my retirement money, pay out money useless and buy an acre of land and issued a phony deed.

If I had issued a phony deed to someone I would be in jail before nightfall.

Therefore you see how the law works. If you are wealthy you will get your due. If you are poor you will get nothing. We need Judges that judge for God and not man.

I used the term crumbling walls to

demonstrate what you see in man could not be good. He might look good, speak well and smile often. You have to look beyond your seeing eye for a standard that will stand forever. The only standard you will find that will stand forever is with God.

If you have a friend, brother which believe this is not true please! Get away from him. This guy is the Devil in human clothes.

One might make fun at this writing but I will tell you something is waiting for you down the road. This is what God said now you call him a liar. If you do your world might crumble before time.

Sometimes our mind might become less understandable. That is when the unpredictability of man arises from hell.

He changes our way of thinking and living. He throws our attention to other countries while he sets us in motion to take over.

He takes our mind off our religious belief

and removes symbols which reflex our God. There isn't much more he has to do.

He must get someone in office to vote and keep us from attending church services. Do not laugh this could happen.

We being praying in school at long as I can remember and that been a long time. I would not in a million years think that would happen but it did. We had Judges for man and not God. That is the difference and should be ashamed to say "In God We Trust".

I thank you for reading

Ralph L. Watts

www.ingramcontent.com/pod-product-compliance
Lightning Source LLC
Chambersburg PA
CBHW030312030426
42337CB00012B/682